I0476072

Sales Secrets For Product Managers

Tips & Techniques For Product Managers To Better Understand How To Sell Their Product

"Practical, proven examples of how to make your customers want to buy your product"

Dr. Jim Anderson

Published by:
Blue Elephant Consulting
Tampa, Florida

Printed in the United States of America

ISBN-13: 978-1501054846
ISBN-10: 1501054848

Warning – Disclaimer

The purpose of this book is to educate and entertain. This book does not promise or guarantee that anyone following the ideas, tips, suggestions, techniques or strategies will be successful. The author, publisher and distributor(s) shall have neither liability nor responsibility to anyone with respect to any loss or damage caused, or alleged to be caused, directly or indirectly by the information contained in this book.

Recent Books By The Author

Product Management

- Product Management Secrets: Techniques For Product Managers To Boost Product Sales And Increase Customer Satisfaction

- Customer Lessons For Product Managers: Techniques For Product Managers To Better Understand What Their Customers Really Want

Public Speaking

- How To Give A Great Presentation: Presentation techniques that will transform a speech into a memorable event

- How To Rehearse In Order To Give The Perfect Speech: How to effectively rehearse your next speech to that your message be remembered forever!

CIO Skills

- What CIOs Need To Know About Working With Partners: Techniques For CIOs To Use In Order To Be Able To Successfully Work With Partners

- How CIOs Can Make Innovation Happen: Tips And Techniques For CIOs To Use In Order To Make Innovation Happen In Their IT Department

IT Manager Skills

- How IT Managers Can Make Innovation Happen: Tips And Techniques For IT Managers To Use In Order To Make Innovation Happen In Their Teams

- Secrets Of Effective Leadership For IT Managers: Tips And Techniques That IT Managers Can Use In Order To Develop Leadership Skills

Negotiating

- Learn How To Signal In Your Next Negotiation: How To Develop The Skill Of Effective Signaling In A Negotiation In Order To Get The Best Possible Outcome

- Learn The Skill Of Exploring In A Negotiation: How To Develop The Skill Of Exploring What Is Possible In A Negotiation In Order To Reach The Best Possible Deal

Miscellaneous

- The Internet-Enabled Successful School District Superintendent: How To Use The Internet To Boost Parental Involvement In Your Schools

- Power Distribution Unit (PDU) Secrets: What Everyone Who Works In A Data Center Needs To Know!

Note: See a complete list of books by Dr. Jim Anderson at the back of this book.

4

Acknowledgements

Any book like this one is the result of years of real-world work experience. In my over 25 years of working for 7 different firms, I have met countless fantastic people and I've been mentored by some truly exceptional ones. Although I've probably forgotten some of the people who made me the person that I am today, here is my attempt to finally give them the recognition that they so truly deserve:

- Thomas P. Anderson
- Art Puett
- Bobbi Marshall
- Bob Boggs

Dr. Jim Anderson

This book is dedicated to my family: Lori, Maddie, Nick, and Ben. None of this would have been possible without their constant love and support.

Thanks for always believing in me and providing me with the strength to always be willing to go out there and be my best for you.

Speaking.　Negotiating.　Managing.　Marketing.

Table Of Contents

You Are In Sales Now!

When you became a product manager, did anyone take the time to mention to you that you were signing up to become a member of your company's sales department? You might have thought that you were joining the marketing department, but if your product doesn't sell, then you won't be holding on to your product management job for long!

Every product manager needs to take the time to discover how to work closely with the members of their sales department. Yes, you control the product, but they control how well it sells and in the end, that's all that matters. Your product is competing for their time and attention with all of the other products that your company wants them to sell. You've got to find a way to get their attention and motivate them.

The sales process is a fixed thing. Customers realize that they have a problem, they go searching for solutions and then they encounter your company's sales teams. When this happens your sales teams have to know about your product. They have to understand how it works. They have to know who it competes against and why your product is better.

No two products are the same. This means that the responsibility of training the sales teams ultimately falls on your shoulders. No matter if you are selling a physical product, a license, or a service, you need to teach your sales team how to sell it correctly.

In most companies, the sales teams won't report in to you. However, you are going to have to build a relationship with them that will allow you to work closely with them. When they encounter a problem or a new competitor, you are going to want them to feel comfortable enough with the relationship that you have built with them so that they'll come to you for help.

In this book we're going to cover just exactly what a product manager needs to do in order to create a working relationship with his or her sales department. We'll discuss how complex sales processes can be managed, how to deal with RFPs, and how extra services can be added to an existing sale.

For more information on what it takes to be a great product manager, check out my blog, The Accidental Product Manager, at:

www.TheAccidentalPM.com

Good luck!

- Dr. Jim Anderson

About The Author

I must confess that I never set out to be a product manager. When I went to school, I studied Computer Science and thought that I'd get a nice job programming and that would be that. Well, at least part of that plan worked out!

My first job was working for Boeing on their F/A-18 fighter jet program. I spent my days programming fighter jet software in assembly language and I loved it. The U.S. government decided to save some money and went looking for other countries to sell this plane to. This put me into an unfamiliar role: I started to meet with foreign military officials in order to explain what my product did.

Time moved on and so did I. I found myself working for Siemens, the big German telecommunications company. They were making phone switches and selling them to the seven U.S. phone companies. The problem was that the switches were too complicated. Customers couldn't tell the difference between one complicated phone switch from another complicated phone switch.

The Siemens sales folks were in a bind. They didn't know enough about how the switches worked to tell their customers why they should buy them. Siemens reached out into their engineering unit looking for anyone who could help the sales teams out. I put my hand up and overnight I became a product manager.

Since then I've spent over 20 years working as a product manager for both big companies and startups. This has given me an opportunity to do everything that a product manager does many, many times. I know what works as well as what doesn't work.

I now live in Tampa Florida where I spend my time managing my consulting business, Blue Elephant Consulting, teaching college courses at the University of South Florida, and traveling to work with companies like yours to share the knowledge that I have about how product managers can make their product be a success.

I'm always available to answer questions and I can be reached at:

Dr. Jim Anderson
Blue Elephant Consulting
Email: jim@BlueElephantConsulting.com
Facebook: http://goo.gl/1TVoK
Web: **www.BlueElephantConsulting.com**

**"Unforgettable communication skills that will
set your ideas free…"**

Create Products Your Customers Want At A Price That They Are Willing To Pay!

Dr. Jim Anderson is available to provide training and coaching on the two topics that are the most important to product managers everywhere: how do I create the products that my customers want and what should I price them at?

Dr. Anderson believes that in order to both learn and remember what he says, product managers need to laugh. Each one of his speeches is full of fun and humor so that what he says "sticks" with everyone.

Dr. Anderson's Product Management Training Includes:

1. How can you segment your market?
2. What problems are your customers having right now?
3. Which of your customer's problems does your product solve?
4. How much of this problem does your product solve?
5. How much will it cost your customer if they don't fix this problem?

Dr. Jim Anderson presents over 100 speeches per year. To invite Dr. Anderson to speak at your event, contact him at:

Phone: 813-418-6970 or
Email: jim@BlueElephantConsulting.com

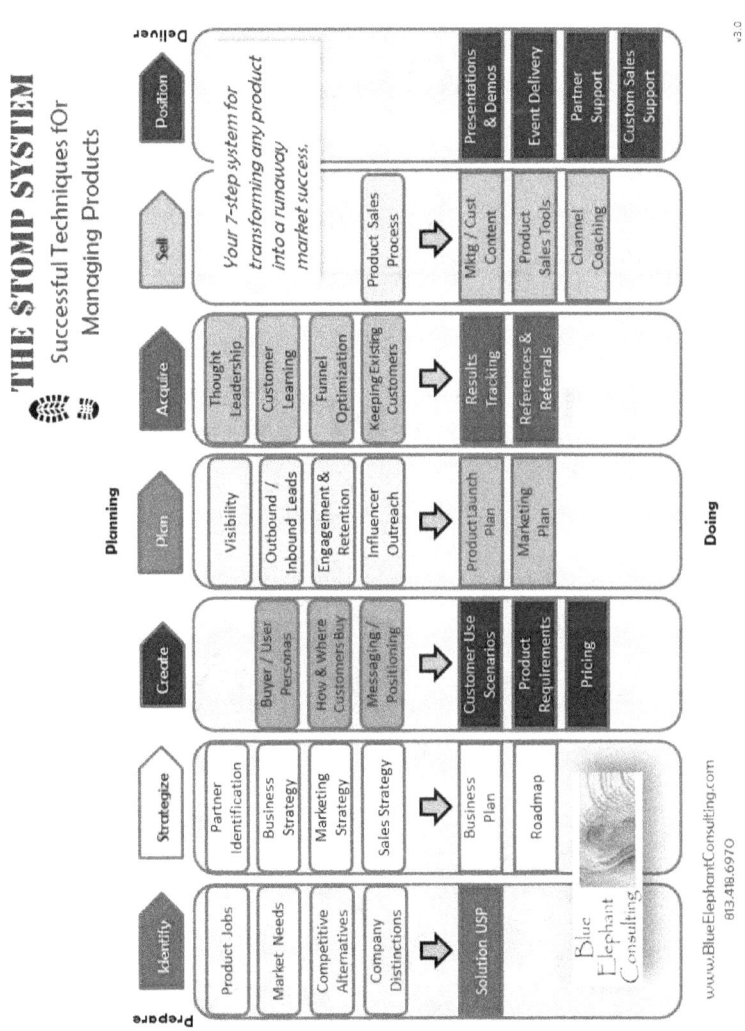

THE $TOMP SYSTEM

Successful Techniques fOr Managing Products

Your 7-step system for transforming any product into a runaway market success.

Prepare				Planning					Doing				Deliver
Identify	**Strategize**	**Create**	**Plan**	**Acquire**	**Sell**	**Position**

Identify	Strategize	Create	Plan	Acquire	Sell	Position
Product Jobs	Partner Identification	Buyer / User Personas	Visibility	Thought Leadership	Product Sales Process	Presentations & Demos
Market Needs	Business Strategy	How & Where Customers Buy	Outbound / Inbound Leads	Customer Learning	Mktg / Cust Content	Event Delivery
Competitive Alternatives	Marketing Strategy	Messaging / Positioning	Engagement & Retention	Funnel Optimization	Product Sales Tools	Partner Support
Company Distinctions	Sales Strategy	Customer Use Scenarios	Influencer Outreach	Keeping Existing Customers	Channel Coaching	Custom Sales Support
Solution USP	Business Plan	Product Requirements	Product Launch Plan	Results Tracking		
	Roadmap	Pricing	Marketing Plan	References & Referrals		

Blue Elephant Consulting

www.BlueElephantConsulting.com
813.418.6970

v3.0

The **$TOMP** product management system has been created by **Blue Elephant Consulting** to help product managers know what to do and when to do it in order for a product to be successful. Contact us for more information on how you can learn more.

13

Chapter 1

How To Work With Sales

Chapter 1: How To Work With Sales

At the end of the day, the whole purpose of any product is for it to be a success. In the commercial side of the house, this means that it needs to be bought by customers and therefore more often than not, you need sales people. What strange creatures they are indeed!

In order for your product to be a success, you need to learn how to work with the folks in sales. Despite what TV and the movies tell us, not all sales folks are like WKRP's Herb Tarlick. Instead, they are almost the complete opposite of your staff: outgoing, people orientated, not always good with details, multitaskers, and often befuddled by technology (but quite good with anything that they need to sell with — like cell phones).

All too often, Product Managers are tempted to stand with the rest of the product crowd and laugh at them. However, you really don't want to do this — you desperately need their support for your product to be a success.

So what's a product manager to do? Simple: spend some time and learn to understand this beast known as sales people. One of the best ways to start is to attend a company-wide sales meeting. These are incredible events and they can be real eye openers.

What you will discover is that a sales meeting is actually a recharging event for sales folks. Engineers look with amazement as sales people hand out awards to themselves and tell each other how great the company's products are and how weak the competition is. What we don't understand is just how lonely a sales job can be.

Product folks get a chance to recharge every day when we interact with our peers — we all acknowledge each others skills and get respect for this. Sales people on the other hand spend their days being told "No" and having their products labeled as too expensive or not having the right set of features. A company sales meeting is how they recharge.

Realizing just how difficult a sales job can be means that a Product manager can change how you interact with sales. If you provide them with material and facts that they can just pick up and use with customers (no reformatting or rewording needed) then you've made their life easier. If you listen to what they have to say about your product and if you show them that their feedback is being worked into the product, then you'll win a friend for life.

Getting the sales team to be on your side is the first step in being the Product manager for your company's most successful product ever...

Chapter 2

Product Managers & RFPs: It's A Love / Hate Thing

Chapter 2: Product Managers & RFPs: It's A Love / Hate Thing

One of the unique things about being a product manager is that we wear many hats during a given day. The sales hat is one that we can find ourselves wearing a lot if our product is new, technical, or just basically foreign to our sales teams.

As we find ourselves in unfamiliar sales territory, one of the jobs that keeps coming up over and over is how best to deal with a Request For Proposal (RFP) from a customer.

Responding to an RFP can take a great deal of time, energy, and effort. That's why it is so maddening when you find out weeks or even months later that some other company won the opportunity or that your proposal was never seriously considered because the customer just used it to drive down the other guy's prices. Arrrgh!

So look, as excited as all of us generally are when we first see an RFP, we really need to understand its background. Your company's sales rep for that account needs to have asked some critical questions.

Is this RFP just being issued so that the customer can do some price shopping before going back to their current vendor and beating them up on price? Or (even worse) is this just a company process that they need to go through and they really have no intention of leaving their current vendor? These are the types of questions that you need answers to BEFORE you start pulling all-nighters to create a response.

If you know your product's competition well, than you can save yourself a great deal of grief. If the customer has already effectively selected one of your competitors and this proposal is just for show, then there is a good chance that the proposal was written with your competition's products in mind and it will quickly show through in the questions that they are asking.

Don't forget your old friend Uncle Google: do a scan of past customer press releases and see if they've awarded contracts to your competition in the past. If so, then re-read the proposal to see if it is slanted towards that competitor.

The best way to make sure that you only spend your time working on RFPs that represent real opportunities is to develop a "Go / No-Go" checklist. This is a checklist that you fill out for each RFP before you start working on it.

The checklist can contain questions like "Does the RFP align with my product offering or my competition's product offering?", "What is the dollar value of this opportunity?", "What is our relationship with this customer?", etc. Once you have all of the answers to these questions, then you can decide if it's worthwhile to respond to an RFP.

Life is strange and sometimes RFPs arrive in the mail (postal and "e") out of the blue. STOP! Before you spend even a minute working on that RFP you or your sales team need to do some digging and find out why your firm got a copy of it.

Make some calls to the company that sent it to you and find out why. Trust me on this – responding to blind RFPs rarely ever results in a sale of your product. Good questions to ask include "How did you hear about my company?", "How many vendors have you asked to respond to this RFP?", "What is the decision making process that you will use to evaluate responses?", "How will you narrow down the list of potential vendors?", and "What are your next steps?".

If you decided to go ahead and respond to an RFP, then it's time for you to do some research. After all of the product information has been provided, there is one final critical section that too many product managers skip over: the request for references.

You need to understand why that request is there: the customer is trying to validate their decision. The more closely matched to the customer that your references are, then the better position your response will be in.

Simple things like providing a CIO as a reference if it's the CIO that is driving the RFP, or providing a firm that is as large or larger as the customer as a reference in order to show that your product works well with companies that are the customer's size.

One last thing: if you don't win the RFP, then by all means call the customer and ask why. The selection process is all over and done with by now and so often times their defensive shields are down at this point and you might get an honest answer if you ask the question nicely.

Chapter 3

Product Manager You Have A Great Product – So Just Buy It Already!

Chapter 3: Product Manager You Have A Great Product – So Just Buy It Already!

As product managers, we are ultimately the source of all knowledge about our products: why it was created, what it does today, and what it will be able to do tomorrow. That being said, we often become part of a sales team when the sales rep has the relationship with the customer, but doesn't understand the product all that well.

This means that we can run into so-called "problem sales" for our products. As awkward as it may feel, this is the time for a product manager to rise to the occasion and help the sales team out. Umm, ok – so now what do you do?

What are some of the problems that you can encounter as a member-of-convenience of the sales team? Here is a common situation that product managers find themselves in:

- The potential buyer really has a need for your product, they have the budget to buy it, and they have been granted the authority to make the purchase.

- Your product / service is the perfect fit for their problem.

- And yet, the buyer does not seem to be willing to make the purchase.

When The Customer Is The Problem: If the customer appears to be dragging their feet, there may be more going on than anyone on your side knows. Big changes like an impending acquisition or money troubles within the customer (like when Wall Street turns upside down!) can cause any sale of your product to slow down or even come to a complete stop.

Interestingly enough, the better the relationship between your sales rep and the customer the more likely the customer will be hesitant to pass bad news ("we're not going to buy your product") on to them. In these cases, it's important to develop another contact within the customer's organization that you can talk with. If the primary decision maker doesn't want to disappoint your sales rep, then this secondary source might be able to provide you with the straight scoop.

When Your Sales Rep Is The Problem: If the customer is unwilling to buy, then the core reason for this is that they simply just don't understand how your product will meet their needs. This means that your sales rep has not been successful in communicating the value of your product to the customer.

In order to fix this problem, more discussions with your customer are required. You need to uncover what their pain points are and then you need to be able to relate your product's features to solving those pain points. Congratulations – if you can do this then you are now a salesperson!

When Your Sales Rep's Boss Is The Problem: This is a tricky problem for product managers to diagnose. What you might not realize is that Sales Managers are often former star sales people. This means that they were good at selling; however, they may not be good at managing other sales persons (gosh product managers: does this sound similar to what goes on in our world?)

Ultimately, the solution to this problem is to have a sit down with the sales rep and his/her boss. I find it easier to blame the product – it's too complex, it's too new, whatever and by doing this it allows the sales manager to feel better about the mess that they may have caused. Generally, they have just confused the situation.

As Product Manager you can step in and offer to talk with the customer to work out all of the "complicated features" of the product. More often than not, the sales manager will be thrilled to have someone clean up their mess. Make sure that you take the sales rep along with you when you talk with the customer so that they can swoop in and close the deal after you've got everything cleared up.

Chapter 4

How Product Managers Can Manage A Complex Sale

Chapter 4: How Product Managers Can Manage A Complex Sale

As a commenter on one of my articles reminded me the other day, we Product Managers are really the CEOs of our product. This means that our ultimate responsibility is to make the product a success.

Depending on your product and depending on your customer, you may occasionally find yourself in the middle of a complex sale. Hopefully you've got a great sales team working at your company; however, even the best sales team is going to have to reach out to the Product Manager to handle a complex sale. Let's talk about what you are going to have to do to help them "land the big one"…

I guess the first thing that we should all agree on is the simple fact that a complex sale is much different than a normal sale of your product. This type of sale is going to require extra preparation on your part, it will probably require a longer selling cycle, and will, of course, require more effort on your part to make it happen.

I've found that complex sales are pretty easy to identify. There is never just one decision maker, rather the product selection process is often spread across multiple departments and may require several levels of executive authority in order to get the deal approved. Nobody said that this was going to be easy!

Making a complex sale happen is really the responsibility of your sales team. However, as the CEO of your product, you care and you have a critical role to play. Here are the three things that a Product Manager needs to do in order to help make a complex sale happen:

1. **Understand What The Real Business Issues Are:** Since you are the Product Manager, you should fully understand what business problems your product can solve. Using this knowledge, you need to learn what the customer's current situation is and determine if there is a match. If there is, then you're going to have to explain this to the sales team in words that they can then use when they are talking with the customer.

2. **Find Out Who ALL Of The Decision Makers Are:** Every company is different and so this question will have a different answer every time. Your sales team may get too wrapped up and focus too much on their point of contact within the company. We all know that, especially for IT products, the ultimate decision maker may have had very little input to the product discussion; however, they are the go-to person that the buyer will double check with before making a decision. It is ultimately your responsibility to keep your eyes open and guide your sales team to talk with ALL of the decision makers.

3. **Determine What Criteria Will Be Used To Make A Product Selection:** Is there a specific business result that the customer is hoping that your product will create? If you can figure out what criteria will be driving the customer's decision making process, then that is where you can equip your sales teams to spend their time showing how your product is better than all of the competition.

Remember, one of the things that the customer is going to want you to really, really understand is just exactly what he is trying to accomplish. If you and your sales teams can do this then you'll be able to win more complex sales than the other Product Managers out there.

Chapter 5

---

7 Ways A Product Manager Can Be A Success During A Recession

Chapter 5: 7 Ways A Product Manager Can Be A Success During A Recession

Psst – don't look now, but it sorta looks like all of the economies in the world are all tanking at the same time. If you are a product manager, this sure does not look good for your career.

I view a product manager as being the CEO of your product and so at the end of the day no matter what the economy is doing you are responsible for making sure that your product is a success. Hmm, if only someone had 7 suggestions for what a product manager should be doing RIGHT NOW...!

Good news – I do. As the CEO of your product you are going to have stand up and take charge even as everyone else in your company may be ducking in order to avoid attracting attention and getting laid off.

At this time you can't afford to be quiet – if your product fails, you'll be gone so you may as well go out swinging. If you are willing to work to make your product a success no matter what, then this list of 7 things that you should be doing is just what the economic doctor ordered:

1. **Get Offensive:** No, I'm not talking about working (more) four-letter words into your everyday vocabulary. Rather, I'm suggesting that you realize that during a recession other product managers are going to be playing defense. They are going to be trying to hang on to the customers that they have because they fear losing them and they're going to not be spending enough time pursuing new customer opportunities. That means that that this recession is a once-in-a-

lifetime opportunity for you to build market share for your product. Work with your sales team and make sure that they are leaving no stone unturned right now in order to find new potential customers.

2. **Incent Your Customers:** Once again, no – don't get them angry; instead, get them motivated to try/buy your product. If ever there was a time to roll out a marketing program that is designed to get those customers who might be sitting on the fence eager to use your product, then this is the time to do it.

3. **Don't Travel:** Within your company, the bean counters are going to be keeping their beady little eyes posted in order to find ways to reduce costs. If you are hopping on a plane every week to go "gather requirements" from customers, all of a sudden you are going to find yourself wearing a nice bright set of concentric circles on you back when it comes time to reduce staff. Instead, use the full power of the 21st Century to reach out and contact both existing customers and new ones that your sales team has found. Although we are often tempted to use email for everything, don't forget to pick up the phone and start calling!

4. **Get Creative:** … with your marketing. One of my favorite quotes from the master marketeer, P.T. Barnum is "Without promotion, something terrible happens … NOTHING!" We're not talking about a big iPhone launch ad campaign here, but rather a whole series of small marketing efforts that can have a big combined effect. Things like free trials of your product, special discounts, or even using the web to set up a

customer portal to provide access to special information and support. Doing an online survey can be a great way to collect valuable customer information while reminding your customers that you are still here.

5. **Talk To Me Baby:** How many times have you been told that an existing customer is 5x cheaper to sell to than getting a new customer? Well, now is the time to put that knowledge into action. Use your existing customers to help drive your product's innovation direction. Collecting this type of information from customers who have already selected your product will allow you to make the product even better which will help capture more market share during the recession.

6. **Retrain Sales:** We product managers know our products inside and out. How well does your sales team know your product? Probably not as well as you do. Use the recession to take the time to bring your sales teams up to speed on what they need to know: new features, planned features, competitive info, etc. Once you've got them pumped up, there will be no stopping them from selling more of your product.

7. **Work Smarter:** When times are good, we all have a tendency to focus on ourselves and try to meet our own objectives. During hard times, we need to instead look at our customers and try to figure out what we need to do to better met their objectives. This may be as simple as adjusting the hours that you work in order to better match your customer and to ensure that you'll be there if they need to call you directly. Little things like this can

make all the difference in ensuring that your product is a success even during a recession.

Chapter 6

A 3-Step Product Manager System To Make Your Product Successful

Chapter 6: A 3-Step Product Manager System To Make Your Product Successful

As the CEO of your product, at the end of the day you are the one who is responsible for it being a success. Not the sales team, not the developers, not the CEO. You.

This is one of the HUGE differences between a project manager and a product manager. Project managers can complete their tasks, make sure that everything is checked off, and then have an immense feeling of satisfaction. A product manager doesn't get to feel this way unless his/her product is a commercial (or internal) success.

At too many companies, the process for making a product a success are way to complex and appear to have been designed by a project manager: they are littered with lots of steps and dozens of milestones. Making a product a success is actually a relatively simple process and a product manager can make it so if you follow the following three steps.

In a nutshell, making your product a success comes down to doing three things correctly: improving the quality of the prospects that your sales teams generate, improving the presentations about your product that are given to potential customers, and increasing the number of potential customers that your sales teams call on. In order to simplify the life of a product manager, improvements need to simultaneously be made in all three of these areas. Now here's how to do that:

- **Improve The Quality Of The Prospects That Your Sales Teams Generate:** Help your sales teams out by getting existing customers to provide referrals to new customers. Hey, the job of selling any product let alone your product is a difficult task. When a salesperson shows up on a new customer's doorstep, do you think that that potential customer is happy to see them? No.

However, if you can get existing customers to open the door for your sales team then the prospect's guard will be down and your salesperson will actually have a fighting chance of getting them interested in your product. Direct your sales teams to only meet with decision makers.

You know better than anyone else what kind of job title is going to be required to shell out the cash needed to buy your product. Tell your sales teams what to look for. This will help your sales teams make the best use of their time – if they can't get access to the right person, they'll know to move on to the next prospect.

Guide your sales team toward the big buyers and away from the little buyers. Every deal takes about the same amount of time to close and if it turns out that a prospect does not have much money to spend, then in reality they are a poor fit for your product. Remember that just a few big deals is much better than a whole bunch of little deals.

- **Improve The Presentations About Your Product That Are Given To Potential Customers:** Help your sales teams out by equipping them with the material that they need for multiple meetings with a potential customer. Rarely will a deal be closed on the first meeting so you are going to have to teach your sales teams about the flow of the conversation as it relates to your product. A key part of this is to help them identify goals for the first and second meetings. If possible, as a product manager you should practice with your sales teams in order to ensure that they aren't repeating themselves due to nervousness nor are they bringing up objections before the customer does.

- **Increasing The Number Of Potential Customers That Your Sales Teams Call On:** You are the CEO of your product. It's up to you to guide your sales teams towards the right potential customers and then let them work their magic. Ensure that your sales teams are only meeting with decision makers – meeting with anyone else will allow your team to be identified as a salesperson instead of potential business partners.

  Have your sales teams take charge of their schedules. Have them agree to meet with a prospective customer at whatever time works best for the customer and then call back later to move it to a time/date that works best for your sales team. This way they can pack more customer contacts into a given day. This is how they will eventually end up selling more of your product.

Finally, make sure that the sales teams that are selling your products are out of the office during prime working hours. If they are in the office, then they are not in front of a customer selling your product and this is bad for both of you. All though this may seem like a lot of sales work for a product manager to do, remember that you are the only one in your company that will ultimately be judged by how successful your product is. You need to be able to do it all…!

Chapter 7

License vs. Sales Product Managers Need To Know The Difference

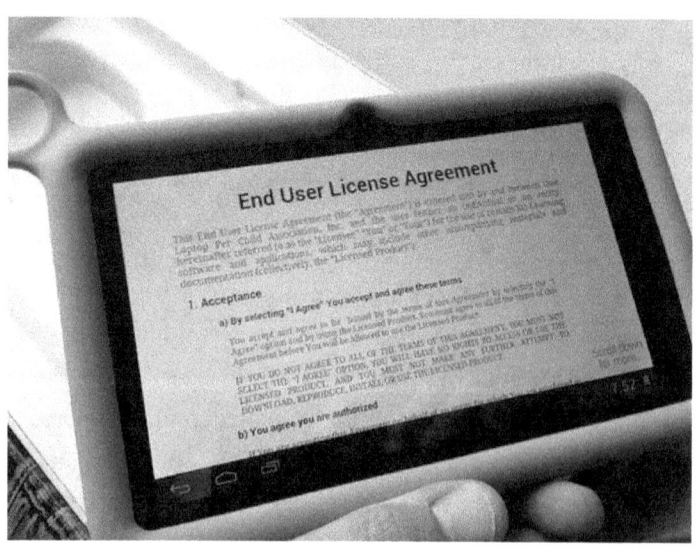

Chapter 7: License vs. Sale: Product Managers Need To Know The Difference

[Note: I am not a lawyer, nor do I play one on TV. I am not giving out any legal advice here. Should you need legal advice, please contact a lawyer in your town.]

In this crazy mixed-up world that we live in, it's the words that can often trip us up. For those of us whose products are software products, often our products come with some carefully chosen words that inform our customers that we have not "**sold**" them our product, but rather we have "**licensed**" it to them. What's the difference?

What's The Difference Between A Sale And A License

In order to sort things out, we need to turn to an expert. In this case, we'll reach out for guidance to Pamela Samuelson who is a Professor at the University of California at Berkeley with a joint appointment in the School of Information and the School of Law.

In a recent issue of The Communications of the ACM, Samuelson pointed out that currently there is **no clear cut court ruling** that spells out if it's legal to purchase a product that comes with a license statement and then turn around and resell it (which is generally what companies who use a license are trying to prevent in the first place).

What Past Cases Tell Us

Just like those lawyers on TV do, Samuelson uses prior cases to attempt to show where things stand today on this issue. In a case called "Vernor v. Autodesk, Inc." a judge ruled that Mr. Vernor could sell some copies of **AutoCAD** that he had bought from a company on eBay.

The reason that the judge said that he could do this was because of what is called **the first sale rule**. What this rule says is that copyright owners do control the first sale of their product (one hop); however after they make that sale, they can't prevent that person from reselling the product (n+1 hops).

What's The Difference Between A License & A Sale

Judges in different cases have really done their homework. In trying to determine if a product that was sold with a license was "licensed" or "sold", they've taken a look at the transaction. Specifically, the law defines **ownership** as meaning that the owner has a right to an **unlimited duration** of possession.

In past cases, this has been found to be the way things were. Additionally, the judges have found that the firms doing the selling have had no interest in having the products **returned to them**.

Final Thoughts

All of the cases in which this has been an issue are still working their way through the legal system. However, if you are a product manager whose product comes with a restrictive license, **you need to be prepared** just in case the courts rule that your customers can resell your product.

The solution to this problem is, as always, a simple one. If your product comes with **a tight relationship with you**, then customers will always want to buy your product directly from you. This is how great product managers make their product(s) **fantastically successful**.

Chapter 8

Offering Extra Services Can Get Product Managers Through Tough Times

Chapter 8: Offering Extra Services Can Get Product Managers Through Tough Times

It's time for some creative product manager thinking. Times are tough, our customers are strapped for cash and yet we'd like to keep sales of our products at least at where they are if not boost them a bit. No matter if your product is a service or a "real" product, there's something that you can do to sweeten the pot for your potential customers – **offer more services.**

Why More Services Work

Even in tough economic times customers **are still buying lots of things**. The trick for a good product manager is to come up with things that will get potential customers off the fence of indecision and onto your list of existing customers. One way to make this happen is to **increase the perceived value** of what they would be getting if they buy your product.

No matter what type of product you are responsible for, a service or a tangible product, you can boost its value by **adding additional services** to what you are offering. When prospective customers are faced with the combined value of both your product and these additional services, hopefully it will be enough to get them to dig out their wallets and make a purchase.

What Types Of Services Should You Offer?

Almost every product already comes with some sort of service offering. Adding additional services should be easy for any product manager to do. Just exactly what these additional services will look like depends on what your product is.

However, here are a **few service suggestions** that will work for most products:

- **Reports**: I personally like offering free reports to my customers because they are viewed as being high value by just about everyone. The reports should be 15-30 pages long (any longer any nobody will read them) and they should deal with a single issue in depth.

- **Consulting Services**: Having access to experts is something that most customers will quickly see value in. Not only will this be seen as an added value, but it may also help to reduce a customer's fear of not being able to get the maximum value out of your product after they have bought it.

- **Videos**: Welcome to the 21st Century – reading is so yesterday. Offering your customers access to videos of some sort, training, demonstration, or interviews with experts can be an instant winner.

Final Thoughts

As is the case with all Product Manager tools, offering extra services to your customers can be a two-edged sword. Product managers need to keep a close eye on your firm's staff – offering additional services can start to **overload staff**. Do this too much and as the economic situation starts to improve you could start to see a company-wide brain drain.

Additionally, your prospective customers could start to **become too comfortable** with your product offerings and may start to expect extra services to be included with all of your products, all of the time. Breaking them of this habit could turn out to be difficult to do.

In the end, product managers need to take the time and do their homework in order to work out the incremental cost of offering extra services. Figure out how to do this and you will have found out how great product managers make their product(s) **fantastically successful**.

Chapter 9

Product Managers Want To Know: Should I Compete Or Create?

Chapter 9: Product Managers Want To Know: Should I Compete Or Create?

In the world of product management, there are a few **"classic questions"**. We all need to be aware of these questions because they keep coming up over and over again during our careers. One such question has to do with what type of market you should plan on selling your product to: an existing market or a new one that you create all by yourself...

Say Hello To Mr. Porter

In the traditional world of product management, we expect to sell our product **in a market that already exists**. This means that as Mr. Porter told all of us back in school, there will be 5 forces at work in that market.

One of these forces will be competitors. This means that we're going to have to spend some time coming up with a plan to make our product **distinguish itself from the competition**. All in all, this is what most product managers are trained to deal with.

Ready For A Blue Ocean Anyone?

In the past few years, a different approach to marketing has shown up. This was probably best captured in the book **Blue Ocean Strategy**. Effectively what this approach is all about is deciding not to compete with other firms and products and instead going out and creating your own market.

What makes this such a powerful approach is that by doing this, you basically **don't have to worry about any competition** until other firms realize what you are up to and start to show up to compete against you. This isn't easy to do, but if done correctly it can be a powerful approach.

Which Approach Is Best?

So here's **the big question**: which way is best for a product manager and your product? It turns out that we're going to get some help here. Dr. Andrew Burke and a team of researchers have been looking into this very issue.

The question that they have been trying to answer is whether a competitive or an innovative strategy will result in **the most successful product**. Their thinking was that if you pursued a "Blue Ocean" type of strategy then you'd end up creating a new market. Naturally, this market would quickly attract other firms. If as this happened, your product's profitability went down as more and more firms entered your market, then you'd know that the new opportunities for your product were probably limited over time.

What The Researchers Found

The researchers found that, not surprisingly, over time competition tends to **erode the profits** that a product manager may have been able to initially make from introducing an innovative product. If there is any good news in this, it's that this erosion takes time. Specifically it takes about 15 years.

What this means for a product manager is that taking a blue ocean approach and creating new markets for your product **may yield the best results**. You can't rest on those results because eventually the rest of the world will catch up with you, but you should have enough time to make generous profits.

The researchers suggest an even better approach. They recommend **a two pronged approach**: creating new markets while at the same time competing in existing markets. This will generate money from competitive markets that can then be used to find and enter more new blue ocean opportunities.

What All Of This Means For You

Product managers need to make important decisions as to what **types of markets** they want to introduce their products into. Two of the most obvious choices include entering competitive markets or creating new markets for your product.

Researchers have taken a look at the benefits and drawbacks of **entering each of these markets**. What they've found is that competition will eventually wear away at your product's profits. This means that creating new markets for your product buys you the most time to make the most profit.

Every product manager will need to make the market entry decision that **best meets the needs** of his or her product and company. However, taking the time to find new untapped markets can yield the best long-term bottom-line results.

Chapter 10

Diversifying To Survive Is What Product Managers Are Doing

Chapter 10: Diversifying To Survive Is What Product Managers Are Doing

It seems almost like an impossible challenge: find ways to constantly make your product(s) both **more popular** (more sales) and **more profitable** (better prices). When confronted with this challenge, it's all too easy for product managers to shrug, throw up their hands, and then focus instead on rolling out the next product or version of an existing product. However, if you are going to survive, then this is a problem that you are going to have to **find a way to solve**.

It's All About Diversifying

It turns out that the key to survival is to broaden your product's appeal to **new markets** while increasing your **profitability** among existing customers. Now these are fine words, but exactly how to do them is the challenge that product managers face.

Knowing **who your current customers are** is the right place to start. Once you have a list of who has bought your product in the past, you can start to do some **segmentation**. More often than not most of your existing customers will have something in common: company size, customers that they are going after, type of products that they sell, etc. Once you know what these characteristics are you can start to identify potential customers who occupy segments that are similar but different.

In order for a product manager's product to be a success, it needs to generate a **profit** when it gets sold and it needs to get sold **as much as possible**. Here are three thoughts on how to make both of these things happen.

- **Cut back on extra services that aren't boosting the bottom line**: this can be a painful and a difficult thing for product managers to do. Over time we keep adding additional services to our products in order to keep them competitive. Over time we lose sight of whether these services are why our customer is buying our product. Often they no longer influence the buying decision and yet they are still costing us money to provide them. It's time to drop them now.

- **Favor Groups Over Individuals**: when you start to focus on your product's bottom line, you quickly realize that it's always better to have more customers than fewer customers. This will serve to insulate you when market downturns occur. To make this happen, sell a single product or service to a group of people for a lower price instead of one higher priced product / service to just a single customer. This may require some product redesign, but it will be worth it in the long run.

- **Maximize Free Advertising**: If you are going to increase your customer base, then the word is going to have to get out about your product. In this era of the social network, one sales fact remains true – people believe what their friends tell them. The group approach enhances word-of-mouth advertising. The more satisfied customers you have, the more free advertising you'll get.

Final Thoughts

Increasing the number of customers that your product has while at the same time boosting your product's profitability is possible to do. The trick is to **diversify** your customer base while **trimming costs** at the same time. I'm not saying that this is easy to do, but if you can find a way to do it for your product, then you will have found out how great product managers make their product(s) **fantastically successful**.

Chapter 11

Product Manager Why Aren't You Doing A Better Job Of Managing Your Sales Team?

Chapter 11: Product Manager Why Aren't You Doing A Better Job Of Managing Your Sales Team?

I don't care if your product turns lead into gold, if your salespeople don't go out there and do a good job of selling your product then you won't be a product manager for long. I'll agree that you are not running the sales department, in fact you are probably not even part of the sales department; however, **your product's life depends on what that department does with your product** so you had better start managing your salespeople.

Walking A Very Careful Line

For those of you who may be thinking "All right, now I've got permission to go in there and tell the sales folks how they really should be selling my product!" I've got one word for you – **don't**.

Sales people are a very different beast from product managers and because of this difference, there is always **the possibility of conflict** when we interact. Our motivations are different (your product is probably only one of many that they have to sell), our time lines are different (you are thinking about the next version of your product and they are thinking about the approaching end of the current fiscal quarter), etc.

The salespeople at your company **already have a boss** – they don't need you to be another one. However, you have a vested interest in their success in selling your product. This means that you're going to have to get clever here.

The Three Keys To Getting Sales To Sell More Of Your Product

In order to start to manage the sales teams that are responsible for selling your product you are going to have to find ways to **work with the sales department** without making it look like you are trying to tell them how to do their jobs.

The first key that you will need in order to be able to do this is to get access to your company's **sales tracking application**. Every company has one of these and if you ask the right people, as a product manager you should be able to gain access to it. Once you are in, you will be able to track how sales of your product are going by sales person, by region, by time period, and potentially even by country.

After looking up some sales numbers for your product, you may be tempted to go running off to sales and start to show off your new-found knowledge by telling them what they are doing wrong in regards to selling your product Once again – **don't**.

You need to realize that sales tracking applications always have at best partial data. The story that they tell is not always correct. If you do see a downward trend for your product's sales, then perhaps **scheduling a lunch** with a salesperson in order to find out what is really going on would be a correct next step (you pay for lunch!)

The Importance Of Sales Metrics

The next key that you will need in order to start managing your sales team is **sales metrics**. The worst thing that can happen is for your sales teams to set their goals for your product without any input from you. A lot of different factors can cause things to change: weather patterns, time of year, market conditions, etc. The factors that affect your product are unique and only apply to your product. You need to work with them to set the sales metrics for your product

Take the time to **identify the metrics** that will affect your product's sales and then share them with your sales teams. Make sure that they know what metrics will impact how they can go about doing their job.

Hands-On Coaching

How did your sales force learn about your product? Did you have a big product launch, throw some product brochures at them and then tell them to go out and sell it? Great – **what kind of success can you really expect from that?**

As part of your product manager responsibility you are going to have to take the time to develop **an ongoing coaching program** for your sales teams. The tone of these coaching sessions is going to be very important. You are not part of the sales department so you need to make sure that you don't come across as sounding as though you are trying to tell them "how to sell".

Instead, what you are going to have to do is to talk to the sales teams in a **supportive manner** that recognizes the challenges that they have and offers them information that will help them to succeed. You are a provider of product and market information, not a sales trainer!

What All Of This Means To You

As a product manager you are effectively **the CEO of your product**. As part of being the CEO it is your responsibility to make sure that the company's sales teams do a good job of selling your product.

Although you don't work in the sales department, managing the sales team that is selling your product is something that you have to do. The trick to this is doing it in a way that **motivates the sales team to sell more** of your product without coming across as being condescending.

You have **three keys** that can unlock the sales team to your message: the company's sales tracking application, sales metrics, and hands-on coaching that you provide. Each of these keys will provide you with additional insight into the sales process and will help you to make your product be even more successful.

Chapter 12

Learn To Read Your Customer's Mind In 3 Simple Steps

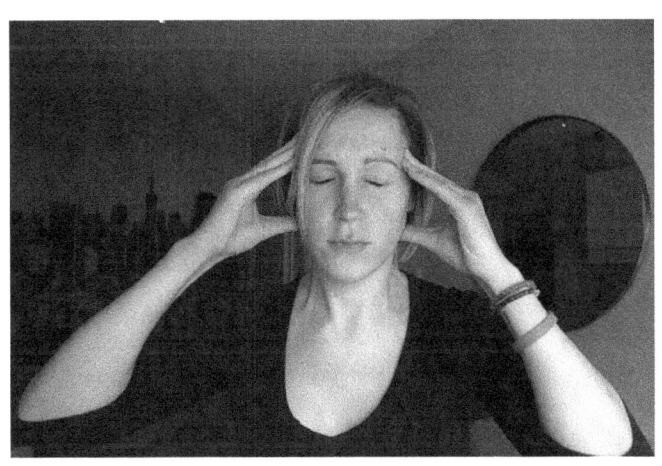

Chapter 12: Learn To Read Your Customer's Mind In 3 Simple Steps

Just shut-up and buy my product! In fact, while you are at it, buy a lot of my product. If only we could really tell our potential customers this then life would be so much simpler. However, try this little verbal outburst just once and then you'll have a chance to sit back and spend some time polishing your resume as you look for your next product manager job.

If you really want people to buy more of your product, then do what I've done – **learn how to read minds**...

How Most Product Managers Equip Sales To Sell

In a recent poll that I took, I asked product managers how they learned to do their job. 50% of the answers were for "on-the-job-training". Clearly most of us are just **winging it**. Since we don't really have any deep philosophy behind most of our product management actions, this explains why most of us are doing such a poor job of equipping the sales teams to sell our products.

If you need a sound bite for what we're doing, then it would be the **"pitch & pray"** technique. This is where we teach the sales teams about the value of our product and then have them go out and pitch it to customers, over and over again. Sometimes it works, most of the time it doesn't.

Moving To The Scientific Approach To Selling Your Product

Not all product managers are stuck at this very basic level of supporting the sales teams. Some of us have seen the errors of our ways and have managed to crawl our way up to the next level: **scientific selling support**.

This is where we've done some research (with or without the sales team) in order to find out just how the customer goes about making buying decisions – what is their **buying process?**

This approach generally brings in many more sales than the old way of just pitching the product's value to as many customers as possible. However, there is one problem: **not all customers are rational**.

The scientific approach of matching your product to the customer's buying process doesn't work in the roughly **33% of all customers** who are not guided by rational decisions. Oh, oh – what to do now?

Top Of The Pyramid: The 3 C's Approach

There is a better way to equip your sales teams to sell your products. I've only bumped into **a handful of product managers** during my career who have been able to achieve this level of collaboration with their sales teams, but the success that they have been able to achieve has always served as a goal for me to shoot for.

At the top of the product selling technique pyramid are the product managers who show the sales teams how they can **collaborate with customers to create new products**. The thinking here is that a potential customer needs more than just your product to solve their problems. If you can teach your sales teams that your potential customers simply don't know what they don't know and that they need to help the customers to understand the big picture of a solution and how your product can fit into an overall solution, then you'll be able to make even more sales.

What All Of This Means For You

Product managers are the **CEO of your product**. In your company, you are the one person who is most heavily invested in the success of your product. In order for the product to be successful, your sales teams are going to have to know how to sell it.

All too often product managers do the minimum amount of work to get the sales teams set up to sell their product: they just outline the product's benefits. What we need to do is to take the **extra steps** that will make our sales teams even more successful. This means starting by taking the time to study and understand our potential customer's buying habits and patterns. Once we know these, then we can help our sales teams match them.

Finally, we can work with sales to help them start to **collaborate more closely with the customer**. Once they are able to do this, then they'll be able to open the doors to both more sales and to larger sales.

Now that you know what you have to do, get out there and help your sales teams to **sell more!**

It's from the forge of failure that the steel of success is formed.

Hard Work Does Not Guarantee Success, But Success Does Not Happen Without Hard Work.

- Dr. Jim Anderson

Create Products Your Customers Want At A Price That They Are Willing To Pay!

Dr. Jim Anderson is available to provide training and coaching on the two topics that are the most important to product managers everywhere: how do I create the products that my customers want and what should I price them at?

Dr. Anderson believes that in order to both learn and remember what he says, product managers need to laugh. Each one of his speeches is full of fun and humor so that what he says "sticks" with everyone.

Dr. Anderson's Product Management Training Includes:

1. How can you segment your market?
2. What problems are your customers having right now?
3. Which of your customer's problems does your product solve?
4. How much of this problem does your product solve?
5. How much will it cost your customer if they don't fix this problem?

Dr. Jim Anderson presents over 100 speeches per year. To invite Dr. Anderson to speak at your event, contact him at:

Phone: 813-418-6970 or
Email: jim@BlueElephantConsulting.com

Blue
Elephant
Consulting

Speaking   Negotiating   Managing   Marketing

Photo Credits:

Cover - By: Kevin Trotman
https://www.flickr.com/photos/kt/

Chapter 1 - By: Mark Hoope
http://www.flickr.com/photos/neonbubble/

Chapter 2 - By: SalFalko
http://www.flickr.com/photos/safari_vacation/

Chapter 3 - By: Michael Holden
http://www.flickr.com/photos/michaelholden/

Chapter 4 - By: carlofaccino
http://www.flickr.com/photos/carlofaccino/

Chapter 5 - By: Anders Vindegg
http://www.flickr.com/photos/anders-vindegg/

Chapter 6 - By: Ayleen Gaspar
http://www.flickr.com/photos/spookyamd/

Chapter 7 - By: Wayan Vota
http://www.flickr.com/photos/dcmetroblogger/

Chapter 8 - By: Joe Penniston
http://www.flickr.com/photos/expressmonorail/

Chapter 9 - By: Tom Raven
http://www.flickr.com/photos/tomraven/

Chapter 10 – By: Kristy Johnson
http://www.flickr.com/photos/kayaker1204/

Chapter 11 - By: Jim Larrison
http://www.flickr.com/photos/larrison/

Chapter 12 - By: Natalie
http://www.flickr.com/photos/nataliejohnson/

Other Books By The Author

Product Management

- Product Management Secrets: Techniques For Product Managers To Boost Product Sales And Increase Customer Satisfaction

- Product Development Lessons For Product Managers: How Product Managers Can Create Successful Products

- Customer Lessons For Product Managers: Techniques For Product Managers To Better Understand What Their Customers Really Want

- Product Failure Lessons For Product Managers: Examples Of Products That Have Failed For Product Managers To Learn From

- Communication Skills For Product Managers: The Communication Skills That Product Managers Need To Know How To Use In Order To Have A Successful Product

- How To Have A Successful Product Manager Career: The Things That You Need To Be Doing TODAY In Order To Have A Successful Product Manager Career

- Product Manager Product Success: How to keep your product on track and make it become a success

Public Speaking

- How To Give A Great Presentation: Presentation techniques that will transform a speech into a memorable event

- How To Rehearse In Order To Give The Perfect Speech: How to effectively rehearse your next speech to that your message be remembered forever!

- Secrets To Creating The Perfect Speech: How to create a speech that will make your message be remembered forever!

- Secrets To Organizing The Perfect Speech: How to organize the best speech of your life!

- Secrets To Planning The Perfect Speech: How to plan to give the best speech of your life

- How To Show What You Mean During A Presentation: How to use visual techniques to transform a speech into a memorable event

CIO Skills

- What CIOs Need To Know About Working With Partners: Techniques For CIOs To Use In Order To Be Able To Successfully Work With Partners

- Critical CIO Management Skills: Decision Making Skills That Every CIO Needs To Have In Order To Be Able To Make The Right Choices

- How CIOs Can Make Innovation Happen: Tips And Techniques For CIOs To Use In Order To Make Innovation Happen In Their IT Department

- CIO Communication Skills Secrets: Tips And Techniques For CIOs To Use In Order To Become Better Communicators

- Managing Your CIO Career: Steps That CIOs Have To Take In Order To Have A Long And Successful Career

- CIO Business Skills: How CIOs can work effectively with the rest of the company!

IT Manager Skills

- How IT Managers Can Make Innovation Happen: Tips And Techniques For IT Managers To Use In Order To Make Innovation Happen In Their Teams

- Staffing Skills IT Managers Must Have: Tips And Techniques That IT Managers Can Use In Order To Correctly Staff Their Teams

- Secrets Of Effective Leadership For IT Managers: Tips And Techniques That IT Managers Can Use In Order To Develop Leadership Skills

- IT Manager Career Secrets: Tips And Techniques That IT Managers Can Use In Order To Have A Successful Career

- IT Manager Budgeting Skills: How IT Managers Can Request, Manage, Use, And Track Their Funding

Negotiating

- Learn How To Signal In Your Next Negotiation: How To Develop The Skill Of Effective Signaling In A Negotiation In Order To Get The Best Possible Outcome

- Learn The Skill Of Exploring In A Negotiation: How To Develop The Skill Of Exploring What Is Possible In A Negotiation In Order To Reach The Best Possible Deal

- Learn How To Argue In Your Next Negotiation: How To Develop The Skill Of Effective Arguing In A Negotiation In Order To Get The Best Possible Outcome

- How To Open Your Next Negotiation: How To Start A Negotiation In Order To Get The Best Possible Outcome

- Preparing For Your Next Negotiation: What You Need To Do BEFORE A Negotiation Starts In Order To Get The Best Possible Deal

Miscellaneous

- The Internet-Enabled Successful School District Superintendent: How To Use The Internet To Boost Parental Involvement In Your Schools

- Power Distribution Unit (PDU) Secrets: What Everyone Who Works In A Data Center Needs To Know!

- Making The Jump: How To Land Your Dream Job When You Get Out Of College!

Tips &Techniques For Product Managers To Better Understand How To Sell Their Product

---

This book has been written with one goal in mind – to show you how to make sure that your product gets sold. We're going to show you how to work with your sales teams to provide them with what they need to sell your product.

Let's Make Your Product A Success!

What You'll Find Inside:

- **HOW TO WORK WITH SALES**

- **PRODUCT MANAGERS & RFPS: IT'S A LOVE / HATE THING**

- **HOW PRODUCT MANAGERS CAN MANAGE A COMPLEX SALE**

- **A 3-STEP PRODUCT MANAGER SYSTEM TO MAKE YOUR PRODUCT SUCCESSFUL**

Dr. Jim Anderson brings his 4 college degrees coupled with over 25 years of real-world experience to this book. He's managed products at some of the world's largest firms as well as at start-ups. He's going to show you what you need to do in order to make your career a success!

www.ingramcontent.com/pod-product-compliance
Lightning Source LLC
Chambersburg PA
CBHW060149200526
45165CB00023B/1418